FORGED BY JOY

FORGED BY JOY

Poems by

Laura Mazza-Dixon

Antrim House
Simsbury, Connecticut

Library of Congress Control Number: 2016959102

ISBN: 978-1-943826-19-3

First Edition, 2017

Printed & bound by Ingram Spark

Book design by Rennie McQuilkin

Front cover: tissue paper collage by Lisa Leach

Author photograph by Wendy Van Welie,
Indigo Images Photography Studio

Antrim House
860.217.0023
AntrimHouse@comcast.net
www.AntrimHouseBooks.com
21 Goodrich Road, Simsbury, CT 06070

This book is dedicated to my mother,
Maralyn June Davis Mazza,
and all the generations before and after her.

ACKNOWLEDGMENTS

Grateful acknowledgment to the editors of the following publications in which these poems first appeared, at times in earlier versions:

From Painting to Poem (Antrim House): "At the Art Show"
Quatrains and Random Thoughts (journal of Laura Mansfield Davis. 1965-1970): "Blue," "To a Candle," and "Of Answers and Questions"
Poems and Essays 2008 (self-published, limited edition)

Many thanks to my mother, Maralyn June Mazza, for the steadfast encouragement and support she has given for years to her six children, her fifteen grandchildren, her extended family and friends. Thanks to Robert Dixon, whose family became so much a part of me over the years we were together. And special thanks to my daughter, Bethany Marie Dixon, whose courage and skill in her own writing of both music and poetry are an inspiration to me.

Thanks to my family and friends, who have served as the first readers and listeners for many of these poems and essays:

To my sisters, Gina Mazza and Susan Van Etten; my brothers, David Mazza and Serafino Paul Mazza; my aunts Jo Davis and Rose Marie Stiffler; and my cousin, Eleanor Mitten-Sapiro, all of whom have welcomed new poems with open arms.

To Jane Bradley and Rosalia Bale, who shared their strength with me until the very end. To Andrea Cleveland Mills, Annie-hannah Mancini, Pat Joy, Sarah Gamble, Denny Moon, Barbara Porter, Sandra Fischer, Helen Beal, Phyllis Merritt, Barbara Powell, Nikki Currie-Huggard, Becky Sears, and the members of the Artist's Way group at South Church in Granby for accompanying me on this journey.

To my musical mentors Judith Davidoff, Grace Feldman, and David Leisner; and fellow musicians Mattie Banzhaf, Linne Landgraf, Ann Carter Cox, Julie Senter, Susan Trump, Anne Mayo, Susan Allen, Douglas Johnson, Susan Lowenkron, Susan Mardinly, Ken Andresen, Nancy Curran, Carrie Crompton, Monika Kinstler, Nat Woodruff, Fred Fenn and Deborah Robin for years spent making music with me.

To my friend Lisa Leach, for agreeing to design the magnificent artwork on the cover of this book, igniting the need for its current title, demonstrating that inspiration flows from written word to art and back again.

To fellow poets Tryfon Tolides, Edwina Trentham, Margaret Plaganis, Nancy Tancredi, Kate Rushin, Richard Wilbur, Jim Finnegan and the Brickwalk Poets for their thoughts on the poems and their friendship, and especially to my editor, Rennie McQuilkin, for his own work as a poet and his willingness to believe in mine.

TABLE OF CONTENTS

THE BRILLIANT ASSAULT

A PRAYER IN SILENCE

NANA AND I

POSTLUDE

PREFACE

I have spent a lifetime traversing the countryside from the mountains of central Pennsylvania and the hills of western Connecticut to the rock-bound coast of Downeast Maine.

Late in the day, when the light falls across the hills that fold down to a river valley, you can see each layer of the landscape outlined all the way out to the horizon. The poems in this book are stories of the play of light and shadow across such a landscape, seen in retrospect, as though from a higher elevation.

Like my Nana before me, I have kept these stories close to me for decades, have puzzled and wrestled and prayed my way through the living of them.

Nana is the one who taught me to see. She taught me to cherish the people and places I loved, and sometimes to write about them.

My ideas about why people write poems go back into my childhood.

Inside the front cover of the book in which my mother's mother copied her poems, she wrote the title *Quatrains and Random Thoughts*. Her name, Laura Davis, appears at the top of the next page, along with a list of those whose poems she would include with her own, poems by her mother, Mabel Mansfield; her son, Donald; and her grand-daughter and namesake, Laura Anne.

It was a book she began about five years after her husband died. The first poem in it is "Alone on a Saturday Night." It is a journal of her life, in verse, and for me, as a young girl, being allowed to copy the poems I wrote into that small composition book was a great honor.

The poem on the next page was one I wrote in fourth grade, for a teacher who commented on it that the color blue was not a happy color, but a sad one. Fortunately for me, Nana saw things differently, and let me write this one in her book.

Blue

Blue is a spruce tree
Standing tall.
Blue is evening
when shadows fall.

Blue is the moon
on a cold winter night.
Blue is feeling
gay and bright.

Blue is the sky
on a hot summer day.
Blue is the jeans
children wear as they play.

Blue is excitement,
Blue is a river,
Blue is when
you start to shiver.

Blue is the dawn
breaking free from the night.
Blue is the ocean
in all its might.

Blue is the wind,
softly sighing.
Blue is when
you feel like crying.

Blue is snow glittering
on a cold winter day,
in which children
happily play.

Blue is a map
showing oceans wide.
Blue is a sadness
you feel inside.

Blue is a spruce tree
standing tall.
Blue is a color
for one and all.

And all the host laughed and wept, and in the midst of their merriment and tears the clear voice of the minstrel rose like silver and gold, and all men were hushed. And he sang to them, now in the Elven-tongue, now in the speech of the West, until their hearts, wounded with sweet words, overflowed, and their joy was like swords, and they passed in thought out to regions where pain and delight flow together and tears are the very wine of blessedness.

J.R.R. Tolkien, *The Lord of the Rings*

FORGED BY JOY

PRELUDE

Curriculum Vitae

Perhaps it will disturb my visitor
to see the way these books
and magazines collect
on and around the bed.

So I will move the books
back onto their shelves,
even though I know each of them
will call to me again,
and land within arm's reach
at the end of another day.

This morning there were
books of poetry by Louise Glück,
whose writing I admire but cannot emulate,
and Tryfon Tolides, a friend
who lives in his grandmother's house
on the side of a mountain in Greece,
where he writes about light and sun
and strawberries in the gardens
of the monasteries on Mt. Athos.

Under one pile, from a few nights ago,
I find a book by Jane Hirschfield,
whose ideas about how poetry works
I eagerly anticipate and read one at a time,
because I know they will burst upon me
like sweet sections of the clementines
I shared with my father in the car last summer
on the way back from the airport in Bangor.

I remember the conversation we had that day.
about all the friends he had lost.
So many gifts, so many friends,
so little strength to mourn each one separately.

So you see how my mind travels
from one thing to another,
and how that might be something
you would rather not know.

Here is Elaine Pagel's book on her research
on the Gnostic Gospels and why
some ideas about the man known
as Jesus were hidden in plain sight,
and others, written on rolls of old paper,
were burned by an old woman
lighting the fire for cooking her dinner.

There are nights I might read one chapter
of one of James Herriot's books
about being a country veterinarian
in Yorkshire, England,
or the second half of an article
I started in an old issue
of the *New Yorker* magazine
during the day and never finished.

My writing of this poem must end now
because when my visitor arrives I expect
she will need clean sheets on the bed
and something to eat.

FIRST THINGS

First Communion

The little pear tree in the backyard
had blossoms all along the branches.

The buds on the grapevines growing
over the arched trellis were getting fat.

Before her Sicilian grandmother tore
the tattered sheet into long strips,
she sat beneath the kitchen window
and shredded the coconut she would use
to decorate the Easter cake she would bake
in the shape of a lamb.

The little girl had been taught
that Jesus was the Lamb of God.
She knew that the next day
she would stand in line
at the front of the church down the street
to receive the bread and wine.

The priest was the only one who was allowed
to hold the holy sacrament of His Body and Blood.
She would keep her hands pressed together, open her mouth,
and wait for him to place the wafer on her tongue.

She could not know if it would be the same priest
who had sat that Friday afternoon in the little wooden box
with the crisscrossing grate at the back corner of the church,
because she could not see him when she made her confession.

She could not remember what she said that day anyway,
because she hardly ever did anything wrong.

As she sat on the piano bench, waiting
for her long, wet hair to be wound
with the strips of cloth, she thought about
the dark suit her grandfather always wore
when he stood at the back of the church
and walked the families to their seats.

Grandfather seemed a little stern in that suit,
and not likely to whistle the way
he did when he was measuring things
with his big folding ruler, or putting the level
up to see if the little golden bubble
was in the middle where he wanted it to be.

On this night, she would sleep all night
at her grandparent's house, in the room
where the lights came through the venetian blinds
and crawled up the wall when the big trucks climbed the hill.

She was surprised to be sent to bed with her hair still wet,
knowing her mother would not approve.

In the morning, she came down the stairs,
and made the sign of the cross with the holy water
in the little metal dish on the wall on the landing

and sat very still on the piano bench,
while her grandmother undid the knots,
unwinding the strips of old sheet one at a time.

Then her grandmother took the new white dress
from the closet and slid it over her shoulders
and zipped it up the back.

Soon her parents and brothers and sisters
came with the new baby
and saw her hair falling in long curls
underneath the white veil
she had been given the day before.

They all walked in the cool air
to the little stone church with the sign
saying Our Lady of Victory
and sat in a row in a dark wooden pew.

When the priest walked into the church
she could feel her hair hanging,
still damp, and a little cold,
down the back of her white dress.

She sat so close to the front of the church
she could hear the latch on the little door
when the priest took the Holy Sacrament
out for communion.

She watched him hold the big wafer
up over his head, and then bless it
and break it into two pieces.

The rest of her family was unusually quiet.
Her brothers were not fidgeting.
Her little sister sat with her legs
sticking straight out in front of her.

Her grandmother had a small veil pinned
to the top of her head, and her mother
wore a little flat hat with a ribbon around the edge.

She looked over at her father once
and found him smiling at her reassuringly.
He had on his dark overcoat and his good shoes.

When it was time she followed the line
of the children from her Catechism class
up to the front of the church.

Her eyes were on the floor
right in front of her
until she reached the priest
standing on the first step
with the wafer in his hand.

When he put it in her mouth
she did not chew it but let it dissolve,
turned to walk back to her seat
and knelt on the cushion to pray.

Afterwards, walking out of the church
and down the stone steps
beside her mother and father,
with her brothers and sisters
all around her,

she stepped over the cracks
in the sidewalk, for good luck,
knew she was different,
but not exactly how.

Summers in Maine

for my mother

Waking on a cool summer morning
with a damp breeze running
through the open window
and birds singing in the tree outside,
I would put one bare foot after the other
down on the blue floorboards
of the upstairs hallway, hoping
to find you already bustling
in the warmth of the yellow kitchen,
a box of berries on the table
and bacon sizzling on the stove.

It was enough to know you
were there, full of plans for the day
ahead, with a pencil and a list
and a cup of hot coffee by your chair.

Those who rose earliest might even
have a little time alone with you,
and hear a story about Henry and Mabel,
or the way Aunt Bert drove her cows
from the big barn by the church
down the road and up to the bay.

Who cared if the next thing would be
getting a job cleaning out the barn or
going to the store for milk and eggs?

Later on, there would be adventures —
finding goats in the field behind the high-school,

visiting Bert Frost at the shipyard, and
climbing on the rocks in the harbor at low tide,
pulling periwinkles out of the rockweed.

With a few cents we could walk past the field
to Tom Alley's gas station and get red licorice,
or up the street to Danny Hall's store
and choose hard candy from glass jars.

If the day turned bright and the fog burned off,
there would be a cooler full of tuna sandwiches
and carrot sticks, and a whole afternoon
spent running on the beach, chasing waves,
and building sand-castles to withstand the tide.

If it didn't, we would get out the monopoly game,
the Parcheesi board and the checkers set,
pull out all the old *National Geographics*
and the *Reader's Digest* condensed books,
and settle in for the afternoon on the rug
and the old green couch in the parlor.

For supper, if it wasn't a corn-hake dinner
with vinegar, onions, salt pork, potatoes
and beet greens, it would be baked beans,
biscuits and corn on the cob,
or, if company was coming,
maybe even lobster straight off the boat
and strawberry shortcake or raspberry pie.

At bedtime, we would all pile onto
the double bed in your room
and Dad would read Ogden Nash poems

until we were falling off the bed,
laughing too hard to breathe.

We would go to sleep in our little beds
tucked in under old quilts, with
woolen blankets to keep off the damp,
all of us sure of our own unique value
and secure in the knowledge of your love.

When we got older, we could be sure
you would be ready to listen
if we needed to talk late into the night
and just as sure you would embrace
every person who showed up at the door,
whether we knew them or not.

The lessons we learned
in that old house in Maine
are the kind that stay with you.

From the texture of those days,
we learned to expect that life
would keep on opening up just like that —
one adventure-filled day after another.

All it takes is a cool grey morning
to bring it all back.

The Honeysuckle Vine

for Peggy Searls

The scent of the honeysuckle vines
outside your front door twines
around all my memories of you.

We were a tribe of hungry kids,
with our skinned knees, muddy pants
sandy shoes and leafy socks,

bicycles, tricycles and wagons clattering
down on the cement of the carport
a signal we would soon crowd into your kitchen
at the end of a long summer's day.

I remember you standing by the stove,
smiling, wooden spoon in one hand,
your house, like ours, open to all.

In the fall, when we gathered apples
from the old tree in the oak barrens
we knew you would put them in a big pot
and turn the heat up until they softened.

You taught us how to press
them through the conical sieve
with the wooden paddle, showed us
how to add the cinnamon at the end.

We knew you loved us, but we did not know
that when you spooned the warm applesauce
into our bowls we were being fed for life.

Trellised on the wind, a sweet reminder
of your kindness drifts over the grey stone wall.

Stone Soup

for my father's 65th birthday

*For what man among you would give
his children a stone,
if they asked him for bread?*

Matthew 7:9

Forgive him, Lord,
With so many of us, all hungry,
what else could he do?

They were small stones at first.
Sea-polished ovals,
green trapezoids laced with gold,

red jasper and yellow quartz,
smoothed like old memories,
filling all twelve of our pockets,
with basketsful left over.

Some we could only look at,
phosphorescent jewels glowing
tangerine, lime and fuschia
in the dark, cool room at the museum.

Others were too big to hold,
giant blocks of pink granite
tumbling on the edge of a continent,

and cream-colored stalagtites
forming drop by drop,
where water never sees the sun.

In time we all grew old enough
to be sent out, first of all
with trusted guides,
eventually on our own.

From one adventure
I came home with tiny pieces
of a Byzantine Messiah
that had fallen through
the golden light to the floor
of the cathedral at Monreale.

My father's sister shared with me
the history of ancient Rome,
and stories of passionate fights

between the Italian sculptors
and the architects whose vision
pierced the medieval night.

One brother traveled to the west,
where he found the mountains,
a youngish range, jealously
covered with snow.

Some say he could hear
what they were saying
in their deep slow voices.

Last time I saw him
he was still trying
to bring them home.

We knew our father
dreamed of the mountains
that had sheltered his family's past,

the stones carved into
the shapes of men
with the faces of angels.

When the time came,
he left his place
in the new world,
guarding the rounded
backs of the Appalachians,

said goodbye to his elderly friends,
the farm families in the valleys,
and the town he knew so well,

and retraced the route
his grandparents took
when they came to America
from the mountains
of Calabria and Sicily as children.

The path he threaded for us
laced the front of the Italian boot,
along twisting roads
cut into the rocky coast
where the mountains
drop into the sea.

He was determined
to bring us with him
to see those ancient stones,
etched not just by water,
but by wonderment and blood.

In Rome, we stood and watched
as he, his boyhood faith restored,
knelt in quiet exaltation

before the brokenness
of one mother and one son,
eternally begotten,
once in flesh and once in stone.

By then, we knew we needed
more than either bread or stone,
and that none of us were fed
if any one remained alone.

Lemon Tree

for Bob

The piazza in Sorrento was full of little tables
where waiters served tiny glasses of limoncello,
casually stepping over the old dog sleeping in the sun
at the restaurant doorway.

The sea lay nearly calm to the west, blue with tiny whitecaps
at the base of a long street sloping steeply down the cliff
to the dock where the boats left for Capri.

Across the street, in the window of a lace shop,
hung delicate openwork tablecloths and napkins
like the yellow ones my grandmother used for her tea parties.

My father sat with the two of us at a table
in the warm October sun
enjoying his limoncello and the view of the water
while the brightly painted little tram full of tourists
went down a street lined with red and yellow flowers.

My mother was having her hair done
in a shop down the way, across from the movie theatre.

My father and I walked back to the pensione,
up the wide red-tiled stairs,
past the old terracotta jars on the landing
and stopped at the ironwork door with the large key.

In the lobby was a table with a bowl of lemons
and a display of plates painted by hand

like the ones my parents gave us for our wedding present.

My father fell asleep almost before he got all the way onto
his bed, still wearing his shoes.

I went back to our room, the one with the bright blue walls,
the low ceiling, and the view of the rooftops out back,
and waited for you.

Ah, Serafino!

for my father

I.

What is life but to fly
across the ocean, board
a train to Venice, stand
on the deck of a vaporetto,
disembark five blocks
from the Hotel Fontana,

pull four suitcases
along the cobblestones
and over the rounded bridges
that cross the canals,
wave to the gondoliers,

walk up to the front desk,
and be greeted like family?

"Ah, Serafino!" exclaims Diego,
calling his grandmother from the kitchen.

"Ah Serafino! Il mio caro Serafino!"

She takes my father's hand and leads him
to a private table, sets before him
a platter of his favorite tagliatelle,

II.

You never met Michelangelo.
Perhaps men of vision, with angelic
names, do not need to meet
to know something of each other.

In the sculpture at the Academia,
Michelangelo portrays David
looking forward with confidence,
standing alone, relaxed,
and ready for anything.

I picture you standing
on the pitcher's mound
with your weight on one leg,
your team arrayed around you
on the baseball field.

David, like you, was a man of faith
and a man of action, willing
to take risks for the things
that were important to him.

He who defended Israel against a giant,
struggled with disappointment
and fought the most difficult battles
with his own despair.

Like you, he treasured
the people and places he loved,
and suffered greatly upon the loss
of his beloved son.

I know Michelangelo must have
had you in mind when he sculpted
the grace and power
lying latent in the sinews
and tendons of David's left hand.

I am only sorry not to have seen
the resemblance in the strength
of those loosely curved fingers,

and the tracery of veins at the wrist,
still warm, until I stood beside you
as your heart joined the heart of
the psalmist, and turned to marble.

GENERATIONS

for Bethany

A Litany of Graces

The wonder of a sleeping child,
a day of needed rain.
The gentle curve of wrist and hand,
a letter from a long-lost friend.

These clouds, swept full of light,
bare-branches sketched
against the early morning sky,
heads bent in prayer, hands outstretched.

The familiar shape of distant hills,
the singing of a song,
an unexpected gift of love,
the way your eyes meet mine.

The moment when you lean against me,
trusting, allowing yourself to rest.
Snow burdening the white pines with beauty,
almost beyond what they can bear.

Mother's Day

In the pre-dawn sky,
the barest crescent of a moon
rises behind the scrim
of this year's new leaves.

The person in the mirror
stands in the half-light,
her body undeniably solid,
its contours reminiscent
of the women
a generation
before and after her.

Among these three women
three dialogues have begun
spiraling across decades
of the past and future.

At no other time will the mother,
her mother, and her daughter
be aligned in just this way.

The sweetness of the blossoms
on the apple trees will last
only a few more days.

I will go into the garden
before the sun is up.

Yesterday

Every tree on every hillside
is in tender new bud.
The hills are swept up in green,
all of it soft.

Dark green pines against clouds of light
green with gold overtones,
green with pink undertones.

The female Canada Goose
glides ahead of her mate
past an island of narcisscus
and over the reflection
of a dozen white birch trunks
and a fragile wild cherry in bloom.

The small girl in the orange and yellow skirt
sits high up on a granite boulder surveying
the masses of flowers spread around her.

She is blonde, three years old,
and basking in the attention
of her mother, grandmother and aunt,
while thousands of daffodils look on.

And now I see my own small one
feeding bread to the Canada Geese at the pond,
curled up reading beneath the weeping cherry,
spinning past the apple tree at the top of the hill.

She is coming up the stairs
with her arms full of wildflowers
and apple blossoms,
her eyes bright with joy;

or striding up the steep trails
behind the farm,
her long legs brown and strong,
the dog racing along beside her.

She is small again, now,
looking up at a little dog on a wall
one street above her in Assisi,

gazing up at the bright colors
of the windows in a cathedral,
light shining down on her head.

Then she is a teenager, looking out
the window of an old house
over a hillside in the Loire Valley
at just this time of year.

She is always looking,
always seeing something new.

On the way home in the car,
I find myself in tears, listening
to *Scarborough Fair*:

"Remember me
to the one who lives there."

Threadbare

In the morning light
of a day in early April,
she folds each one
of the old washcloths
to make a soft stack
on the windowsill.

Outside the window,
the snow melts
into a muddy trench
and down the slope
of the broad hill.

The sun slants through
the swamp to the east,
brushing the bare branches
of the Japanese maple
with ochre light.

The maple tree was planted
to mark the birth
of her only child, a girl,
born the same week
the trillium opened
at the edge of the woods.

Soon the buds
of the maple will open
into pairs of scarlet wings
and be sent out into the world
by the thousands.

The Red Tulip

The other day I passed
a tall red tulip standing
by itself along the roadside
and thought of you,

a young girl in a green dress,
back straight, head held high,
crossing the recital stage,
determination in every step.

The bulbs I planted
the fall before you were born
wintered over during
long months of dreaming.

In the light reflected by the snow
I laid bright squares of cloth
in patterns on the dark table,

joined them with narrow seams
into rows of diamonds
to cushion the sides of your crib.

I watched the bulbs sending
up shoots, and then buds,
as the days grew warmer,

and rejoiced with the chorus
of seven tall red tulips
that opened the week you were born.

The last time I saw you,
a fierce desire for independence
burned in your gaze.

Your eyes held a plea as well,
one you would not acknowledge.

When you turned away last fall,
striding down the grey streets of London,
in your red winter coat,
shoulders squared, I knew you were gone.

You are a young woman now,
strong in spirit, but still fragile;
my days are full of your absence,
my nights lost in concern for you.

So, when I found the red tulip
lying in the grass yesterday,
its stem broken off at the base,
I could not leave it there.

I brought it home with me,
filled a small glass vase
with water from the tap,
set it on the kitchen windowsill.

The tulip's satin petals,
veined deep red on red,
respond to the light.

I watch it opening
in the morning
and closing at night.

I remind myself it is not mine,
though I admire it.

I say a prayer for myself
for wisdom, while I learn
to give you room to breathe,

and a prayer for you,
for protection, while you learn
to stand alone.

Things That Remain

I found the shards of your project
from pre-school lying scattered
across the floor this morning.

Scowling at the orange cat,
whose business it is to find
things that can be broken
and break them,

I bent in grief to retrieve
the pieces, and found that

the three small shells
that had been embedded
in white plaster,
were now free.

I stand by the window
in the afternoon light,
with the three small shells
in the palm of my hand,

reading the poem
you have just written,
a gift which allows me
a glimpse of your resilience.

I am grateful for this reminder
that the most precious
things cannot be broken

and sometimes are freed
when what holds them
breaks open.

The Return

Even at mid-day in the heat of summer,
here, where the brook slows and bends
to pass the granite shoulder of Broad Hill,
the air will always be cool.

Here, the pool will be still enough
for skimming dragonflies to draw concentric circles
that overlap and widen across its dark surface.

Here I stand and wait, watching
as the hatchling trout dart just below the surface,
remembering two small girls at play,
laughing, small bodies glistening.

May the memory of this stillness,
and the currents running deep beneath,
be a sanctuary to which you can always return.

Coming Home

I am in the audience for a concert
at the library my brothers and sisters
and I visited as children to find books
to read when the fog rolled in.

I remember opening the heavy front door
of the vestibule, the excitement of looking
for the adventures of Nancy Drew
and the Hardy Boys,

the librarian at the desk smiling
as she handed us the oaktag slips
where we wrote our names in pencil
for the books we found.

The three-masted schooner, sails billowing,
still rides the blue-grey waves in the painting
in the ornate frame that hangs on the wall
above the piano.

Ships like those were built in this town
and still sailing one hundred years ago,
when this library was new.

I think back to a poem that my grandmother,
a young girl in those days,
wrote years later —

Again I saw the big white ships,
Made here so long ago,

With cargoes for some far-off port,
And Captain's families, restless to go.

As I, a little girl of ten,
Watched the ship disappear
"Why could Helen Lamson see the world?"
Thought I, holding back one tear.

Since that day on the Coast of Maine
Much of the world I've seen,
but never quite with the longing
of that little Maine girl's dream.

Now, my daughter, her great-granddaughter,
steps forward and smiles at the audience.

She sits on the bench at the old upright piano
in a cotton dress of soft yellow,
printed with garlands of pink and yellow roses,
and cinched by a wide leather belt.

She wears a small straw hat trimmed
with the same fabric as her dress,
its soft brim folded back over her brow.

Her outfit is one my Nana might have
worn when my mother was a child,
the songs she sings ones my mother
loved when she was first in love.

The music of the 1930's and '40's is the music
chosen for this concert, which is dedicated
to my father. Bethany opens with "Georgia"
and "What a Wonderful World," two of his favorites.

The audience is of my parents' generation,
many of them their friends, and I hear them
humming along with "Honeysuckle Rose,"
"Moon River," and "The House of the Rising Sun."

My mother sits with her cousin Bonnie
and her friend Helen in the front row.
They have each lost their husbands recently,
and all three of them are dressed in blue.

But when my mother gets up at the end
and joins Bethany to sing a duet
of "The Blue Juniata,"
none of us can stop smiling.

ARTISTS AT WORK

New Year's Day

The year is off
to a slow beginning.

A day of steady rain
and small tasks.

An evening beside the fire,
my dog at my feet.

And now, the opening notes
of the aria from Bach's
Goldberg Variations,
the one I want played
at my funeral.

I close my eyes
and see the composer
wrapped in a coat and scarf,

lost in thought
as he walks down a path
to a grey stone church.

His head is down,
his shoulders stooped.

The first note sounds,
low in his throat,
an absent-minded accompaniment
to his deep deliberations.

The second, at the same pitch,
and of equal duration,
the simplest response to the first,

as though he is humming,
agreeing with himself.

Two quicker notes ascend
as he places his hand
on the railing, his left foot
on the first stone step.

By the time he climbs
one step higher,
the meter has been set,

and as he shifts his weight
back onto his right foot,
the notes proceed in reverse,

with a graceful descent
that ornaments the triad
on the dominant.

Bach pulls the heavy door
open and steps inside
the silent church.

His pensive mood
has not passed,
but it has found a voice.

By the time he has reached
the nave and thrown his overcoat
on the nearest pew,

the figure that will serve
as answer to the first
has risen from his heart,

and he has begun to sing.

Chaucer's Nephew

for Rennie

His habit of listening
as he walked alongside
the other pilgrims,
his head down, eyes on the path,
made it possible for him
to observe them privily.

There was no need
for a disguise, for he too
sought solace in that journey,
suffered damp and hardship,
carried questions in his heart
too heavy to bear alone.

And so it was that from those
struggling to keep up, he learned
something about perseverance,
and from those who suffered,
something about courage.

Some fellow travelers still remember
the man with the steady stride,
the one who shared his own tales
as they gathered close together
around the fire in the evening.

Home from the pilgrimage,
and long afterwards,
he contemplates the fire

burning on the hearth.
His gaze, still clear, turns inward,
and he follows the path again.

The stories of those he encountered
along the stony path, he stacks,
cord by cord, inside his heart,
fuel for the next journey.

The Lady and the Unicorn

The grey stone walls of the small underground chamber
at the Cluny Museum in Paris are warmed by six ancient tapestries.

In each one, a royal lady, a lion and a unicorn interact
against a background of flowers woven into a red field.

In some of them, the lady's handmaiden appears as well,
but she is not in attendance in this one.

Here the lady sits on a bench outdoors,
with an oak tree on her right and a holly on her left.

Many bright wildflowers have been knotted into the grass
where two rabbits and a small spotted dog play at her feet.

The unicorn sits to her left, with both front hooves in her lap.
He has turned the burgundy lining of her overskirt inside out.

With her delicately embroidered skirts in disarray,
the lady looks down and to the side in a melancholy way,

while he admires his long horn and his dashing goatee
in the ornate mirror she holds in her right hand.

Her left hand lies along his neck, tangled in his white mane,
where she has been stroking him absent-mindedly.

The young lion who bears her standard, three crescent moons
rising diagonally across a blue banner, averts his eyes.

At the Art Show

The paintings are numbered
and hang next to each other
on the library walls.

Six harbors, a stone wall,
three horses, one with a girl,
two dogs, an old couple seen from behind,
a baby, a field of red poppies, and a bowl of lilacs.

On Tuesday evening,
the ladies of the poetry workshop
come to study the paintings and to write.

"Jump off from here," he says.
"Go where the poems lead you."
I guess we trust him; he says he has been there.
So, as a group, we go. We jump.

Some of us prowl. Others stake a claim.
Attracted to the falling light here
and bold splash of color there,
we eye every shadow and the line of each horizon.

We are no longer spectators. We are at risk.
The artists are gone. They have distilled
their vision here. Now it is our turn.
We must go further.

Restless and wary, we ignore each other,
staring pointedly into the distance,
as though the room has grown too small.

We bend our heads over our notebooks.
The room fills with a deepening silence
while night gathers outside the windows.

When we read our work, the silence breaks
with the shock of grief and loss.

The room begins to resonate
with voices not yet heard.

At nine-thirty, we leave the room,
realizing how little we understand
about each other, how alike we are.

These landscapes are within, inviolate,
the journey just begun.

The paintings hang untouched.
At least they appear that way.

Henri and the Scissors

after the Matisse exhibit
at the Museum of Modern Art

In the chapel at Vence,
an old man sits
in a chair by the window.

A young woman
in a dark blue dress
stands behind him
in the shadows.

With a heavy sheet
of painted paper
draped over his left hand,

he takes the long scissors from her,
lifts the edge of the paper,
and begins to cut.

As the scissors open the edge
of an undulating line,
the paper comes alive
in his hands.

Now the paper is a puzzle
twisted around itself;
now it is tangled
like a young girl's curls.

It is about to fall
but the old man
never lets it go.

He continues to cut,
slowly, deliberately,
lifting the paper
over and over again,

until the scissors
emerge at the edge
where he began.

Miraculously, the paper
is still all of a piece.

He holds it up to the light
with both hands,
a branching coral,
a sea creature.

The young woman steps
out of the shadows
as he hands her
another living being

to place against
the darker paper
hung upon the chapel wall.

Da Pacem

Arvo Pärt had reached a position of complete despair in which the composition of music appeared to be the most futile of gestures, and he lacked the musical faith and willpower to write even a single note.

Paul Hillier

I.

If I sing just one note
and then refuse to relinquish it
when you sing another note
very near to mine,

we will sound as though
we are at war.

The truth comes to us all
in the same way,
riding on the interval
of a minor second,

entering our world
at the point
of unbearable dissonance.

If this is the way
God speaks to us,
no wonder we are afraid.

II.

Each pitch is carefully placed in position
like stones in a Zen garden. / Paul Hillier

A composer living in a country
where both the practice of religion
and the performance of his music
were forbidden,

Arvo Pärt sought solace
in silence and the study
of ancient sacred music.

When he emerged to write again,
he set the most dissonant
of harmonic intervals,
the minor second and the tritone,

in the upper voices of the choir,
a restless shimmer
of unresolved dissonances

above the lowest notes
of the organ, sustained

as firmly as the stepping stones
in a Japanese garden,

creating sacred sonic space
in which tragedy and discord,
though ever-present,

are encompassed by grandeur.

THE BRILLIANT ASSAULT

Fall Garden

The summer my friend died all I could do was dig.
I filled wheelbarrow after wheelbarrow with sod,
the exhaustion an antidote to grief.

I moved her favorite perennials
into the new garden, divided the bleeding heart
and the French lilac, and planted them
beside the white azalea.

With a trowel I loosened the shallow roots
of the forget-me-nots my mother had saved
from my grandmother's garden in Pennsylvania,

carried the small bundle of leaves and seedpods
to a new home near the rosebush,
and pressed them gently back into the ground.

The year my brother died, my father
and my brothers dug his grave by hand,
beside my great-grandfather's grave
in the cemetery on the coast of Maine.

We stood under the birch trees on the hill,
took turns placing around the urn
handfuls of the smooth stones of jasper
we had collected in blueberry boxes as children,

watched as his young daughters and their cousins
picked stems of Indian paintbrush and daisies
to go in the grave, and took turns with the shovel

until the stones and the flowers
and the urn holding his ashes
were blanketed by the soft peat soil.

That summer I worked in the garden
overlooking the harbor, under his favorite tree,
surrounded by the lupine he loved.

When summer ended I brought the seedpods
back with me and shook the seeds
out of the dry pods over the whole bed,

marveled the following year when the lupine
flourished in the heat of the Connecticut summer.

The Brilliant Assault

I took offense,
the year she died,
that summer's green
should be forged into gold.

When the birches on the hill
began polishing their swords,
I looked away,

refused to admire the rosehips
ripening by the pasture,
took no joy in the late strawberries
or the miniature constellations
of wild asters by the old stone wall.

I steeled myself
against the alleluias
ringing from each bronze leaf
beneath that lapis sky.

I suppose I should have joined them.

"No, not this year," I thought,
"Not so soon.
Not now."

Instead, I hardened my heart
against my favorite maple at the corner,
and walked right by,
pretending not to care.

Another day, or two,
of such relentless glory
and I might have been defeated,
my heart pierced by swords of joy
on every side.

Can joy weigh more than grief?
I can't decide.

But never mind, the question's moot;
the brilliant assault is nearly over now.

Discarded weapons lie in drifts, tarnish
edging each cunning curve and point.

See how the news flies south?

Wings beat victory over and over
against the knowing sky.

Trampling the last crimson daggers
to a rustle along the road,

I wonder if it would have been
better to have lost.

Monday, October 16

I

That afternoon I found myself in the garden,
pulling seed-bearing violets up by the roots,
raking soil around the base of the rosebushes,
making a place to plant the lupine seeds.

An unsettling concern had driven me outside.

There was no wind, but the air around me
seemed to fill with many sets of mighty wings,
accompanied by an insistent, nearly frantic,
sense of something needing to be done.

I could not find the source of the disturbance.
Not knowing what to do, or for whom,
I set to weeding the end of the garden
that was still in the sun, my heart pounding.

In an hour it was over. The air was calm.

II

The next day, I drive to the nursing home,
Rosegarden, to visit the newly bereaved widow
of my husband's Uncle Cylime.

She lies on her side, his wife of sixty years,
her back to the empty bed beside her,
her rosary beads wrapped around her left hand.

We talk about how she thought he would be back,
how she is too weak to pray.
I tell her I will pray for her, she who prays
for everyone, including the priests.

On the wall by the window, where the smooth
sheets are pulled up over his empty bed,
I find the painting we gave him years ago.

The trees are bare, the woods still full of snow,
but now it seems to have come to life.

The ice is breaking up on the Machias River.
Crystal blocks thrown aside by the current
collect among the logs jammed on the riverbank.

Upriver, the dam must have been opened
and the logs cut during the winter released.
Now the river drivers are hard at work.

They stand astride the logs
in the thunderous whitewater, balancing
and running from log to log, using long poles
to drive the logs downstream.

III

The tumult in the painting reminds me so much
of the disturbance that overwhelmed me in my garden
that I suddenly think I understand.

I believe the old lumberjack who died so recently,
alone, unnoticed, in a hospital bed,
the man with the soft heart and the gruff voice,
was looking for company in his journey downstream.

If so, he found me in the garden that I'd dug by hand
the year my close friend died of cancer,
the garden where the memories of my brother
are planted every fall with the lupine seed.

Acquainted with Grief

At first, time stops.

Our expectations
shatter around us.

Words come later,
if they come at all.

Unprepared, we inhabit
the silence of disbelief,
our awareness of the truth
delayed, arriving like
thunder after lightning.

In the moment,
all is restless agitation,

as though it were possible
to turn quickly enough
to catch a glimpse
of what has been
irretrievably lost.

That opportunity past, we try
to keep the earth from turning,
slow the way the day
swings across the sky

until we fall, exhausted,
not choosing to rest,
but resting nonetheless,

waking in a place
like twilight, greyer
than the dawn, marked
by neither day nor night.

Etude #5

I.

The room we were in was barely big enough
for me to set up a chair and a music stand
near the door that opened onto the hallway.

I had gone to St. Mary's Hospital to play
for my husband's Aunt Edwidge
many times before, because I knew
the music helped her feel more calm.

On this afternoon her breathing
was ragged, coming at uneven intervals.

Her sister and her daughter
sat on either side of her,
each holding one of her hands.

II.

Aunt Edwidge grew up in northern Maine.
She was known for her strength
digging potatoes as a young girl.

At fifteen she crossed the Madawaska
on a wooden bridge so she could get a job
working at the lumber mill in Stockholm,
bought a company house for fifteen dollars.

She was twenty when her mother died.
Men carrying lanterns walked beside
the horse-drawn wagon that carried
her mother's casket down the hill
to the crypt to be stored until spring.

Aunt Edwidge married a lumberjack
and lived on Charette Hill,
lost her first baby at three weeks
and her second at ten months.

Two more children were born
before she and her husband moved
to Connecticut. Her sisters came as well
and stayed in her house.

The men found work at American Brass,
the women in the Timex factory,
painting radium on the watch faces,
licking the brushes as they went.

During the war she worked in the brass mill
but was laid off when the men returned from war.

Aunt Edwidge was a fast worker, and a good one.
She got a job at Scoville's buffing lipstick cases
in the shop where grenades and fuses
had been made during the war.

After her husband died of emphysema
she saved up her pin money to take dancing lessons.
She loved to tell the story of how she "got cold feet"
when she reached the top of the long flight of stairs
that led to the Arthur Murray Dance Studio.

She was all ready to go back down when
the dance teacher encouraged her to come in.

Her oldest son was murdered at thirty-one
by a jealous motorcycle gang member.
Another son was hit by a drunk driver,
lost one leg, and died of heart failure at fifty-three.

Aunt Edwidge nursed a grandson at her house
after his heart transplant,
taking a bus to the drugstore for his medications,
but lost him later than year.

No matter how difficult life became,
she and her sisters stayed close.

Dancing proved to be one of her delights
later in life, especially with her partner, Able,
who kept company with her at many family
gatherings and games of cards at her house.

Aunt Edwidge crocheted an afgan for me
when her nephew and I were first married
and gave me an embroidered tablecloth
one Christmas, a family heirloom.

In early spring, she and Able would gather
fiddlehead ferns to share with us.

When we visited, she always greeted us
at the door in her apron, welcomed us
into the big kitchen with the linoleum floor
and offered our little girl a cookie.

Aunt Edwidge invited everyone to her house
for Thanksgiving, and when we arrived
she would be at the kitchen table, peeling
the big yellow turnips to mash with butter.

Ten of us sat in her front room at a table
over the grate where the heat came up from below
and listened to jokes about the cooks
in the lumber camps in Maine.

III.

My dog-eared copy of the fifth piece
in Andres Segovia's edition of
Twenty Studies by Fernando Sor
is missing the bass note for the last chord.

I approach the last few measures
with care, allow the tempo to slow,
listening to the way the notes increase
their distance from each other,

aware of the increasingly long
interludes between Aunt Edwidge's
coarsely textured breaths.

As I reach the final chord, careful
to play the missing bass note for it,
I realize something else is missing.

Aunt Edwidge has not taken another breath.
That silence is with me still.

A PRAYER IN SILENCE

Without

on the occasion of Donald Hall's reading
after the death of his wife, Jane Kenyon

I

Within these curved stone walls
the community of poets gathers
on the slope above the old gazebo.

The garden is filled with roses
and sweet woodruff, the air soft
with the dusky smell of lavender.

This evening we arrive carrying
our own losses along with
our blankets and our chairs.

It is a perfect summer night,
but in this unforgiving light
every face seems etched with sadness.

Like driftwood stripped of all sweetness
after long years of weathering
the salty assault of the open sea,

we sit exposed to one another's gaze
in the low, late August sun.

I am learning what it is to lose,
wondering what storm has driven
all of us ashore at once.

II

Now, as the poet at the heart
of the garden sounds aloud
his litany of despair,

we are united by
the sorrow that we share.

He was your companion
when darkness held you prisoner.

He rejoiced with you
when contentment appeared
as a welcome guest
and happiness surprised you both.

As he speaks your words, Jane,
we hear your voice again.

From the center of this garden,
you speak of finding beauty
in the midst of sorrow.

Gently, you remind us,
as the sun sets and darkness falls,
our common ground is grief.

We walk with you
through the fields you love,

stand with you at the door
of the shed at nightfall, listening
to the cricket and the owl.

for Jane Kenyon

Peony Season

for Cynthia

In every vase
of every shape and size,

the heavy tower of cut-glass,
the short, half-round green one,

and the hand-blown amethyst
one with pressed-in sides
from my mother's mother's house,

the peonies in bud and bloom
will grace the house
for these few weeks,

and then allow
their delicate petals
of pink and white
and burgundy

to fall away
in translucent
drifts,

leaving
a star-burst
on every stem.

On Orchard Hill

We've just arrived.

Why fill the bag
so quickly?

The sky is close
enough to touch.

The trees in the field
are full of apples

shining red
against the blue,

like Christmas apples
in a children's book.

See how they bend
the branches down to us?

Stand longer with me
near the tree by the road.

I know the sun
is in the west.

Stay here.

Tell me another
new thing.

Disturbing the Lavender

Herbs tend to be tough by nature,
and that is why they are such gratifying
garden citizens. They give and give.

Stephen Orr, *The New American Herbal*

The lavender on her doorstep
has survived the winter once again,
but not without complaint.

I never can resist the temptation
to reach down and break off
a few of the soft grey-green leaves,

spin them gently between
my thumb and my fingertips
until they release the scent I love.

The friend who greets me at the door
has spent her long life dedicated
to the things that matter:

discipline, posture, articulation,
hand position, French pronunciation,
punctuation and grammar.

Drawn by her attention to detail
I have been bold enough to approach,
disturbing her solitude again and again
to learn lessons about keeping one's focus,

sharing conversations
about teaching music, writing, painting,
birds, children, grandchildren, and gardens.

Now she rests against the cushions of the sofa,
the upholstery a deep orange
with tiny suns of gold scattered across it
like photos sent back by a telescope in space,

shocked that the students narrating
Saint-Saëns' *Carnival of the Animals*
could not pronounce the composer's name.

It will be up to someone else
to correct such errors now.

Lost in a book about the kings
of England, she will not show me
her last painting, nor the murder
mystery she wrote years ago.

At her request, I ask no more questions.

Her eyes close against the pain
while I gather tools from the shed,
plant pansies in pots to place
on the flagstone beside her front door,

set primroses in beds along the deck
beneath the hemlock tree
where she hangs the bird feeders.

I close the door quietly.

A Prayer upon the Moon Setting

The moon was rising full
when I went to sleep.

Wakened early,
by a sky as bright as day,

I find the moon poised
in golden perfection
above the dark sweep
of the wooded hill.

I take up my seat
by the window
to watch the moon sink
behind the familiar ridge
and disappear,

a private ritual to honor
the balance between
the darkness and the light,
and the riches revealed by each.

On this night, I find myself
calling out for the moon to stay
as it sinks lower in the sky.

It does not hear me,
continues its relentless descent,
abandoning the little valley,

leaving no trace of light
in the cloudless western sky.

The times when the moon sets
just as the sun rises
are the ones I wait for all year.

This will not be one of them.

Without the golden glow
of the moon, the late winter
landscape lies still and sere.

The dreams from which
I awakened seem to have
abandoned me.

I light a candle, remind myself
to be grateful for the moments
in between each day and the next,

hold a prayer in the silence
of my heart . . .

May the richness of the night
be made manifest in my life
as the day begins.

NANA AND I

Wildflower Gardening

I.

Their names had taken root in my imagination months before
the packages of seeds arrived by mail.

Star-flower
Blood-root
Rue anemone

I had memorized the drawing and the description of each flower
on every page of Johnny's Seed Catalog and mapped out where
I would plant each one in the circular bed in my grandmother's
backyard.

She had given me permission to plant my own garden at the base
of an oak tree behind her house on North Oak Lane.

Nearly all the trees were oaks in the woods where I spent my days
exploring and dreaming with my five siblings and my best friend
Andrea.

I knew how to find the glossy green leaves that hid the ripest
teaberries. I knew that the Indian Pipes were more likely to
appear after a heavy rain. Andrea and I had sworn each other to
silence over the place we had seen the pink Lady's Slipper even
though my brothers could have spotted it from their tree-house
if they had been paying attention.

So I had a plan. I would grow a wildflower garden.

Nana started her seeds in trays by the kitchen window in the
wintertime.

Delphinium
Larkspur
Cosmos

They were beautiful, but ordinary.

I had made up my mind. My garden would be different.

II.

When the ground had warmed enough to loosen the soil around
the roots of the oak tree, I carefully opened the packages of seeds
and planted them according to my plan.

When I was very small, Nana had taught me how to "put them
to bed." So I patted the soil down gently and was careful to give
all of them enough water, but not too much.

Then I waited.

Every day, I walked up the hill and through the neighbor's back
yard to check on them. I knelt on the grass and searched my
garden for signs of life.

Some of my seeds came up, but not all.

I could spot the delicate leaves of the rue anemone, and the
heart-shaped leaves of the yellow dog-tooth violets, and finally,
the feathery ones of the Dutchman's Breeches.

But no painted trillium, and no star-flowers.

What I learned, and have had to learn many times since, is that
things do not always go according to plan.

I learned that wildflowers are called wild flowers for a reason. They will grow only when the conditions suit them, and only where they choose.

I have seen them growing in the most unlikely places – Scottish bluebells nestled in the crevice of a granite outcropping on the coast of Maine, bloodroot coming up through the old leaves along the side of a dusty road.

So when my mother appeared in my bedroom, years later, holding a stem of deep red trillium the week my daughter was born and said she had found it in the woods at the end of the driveway, I caught my breath.

I knew enough to be grateful. I knew I could walk down to see the trillium growing at the edge of the woods.

It was, and is, a gift.

But I also knew enough not to disturb it.

III.

I loved my little garden, and I have loved every garden I have planted since.

When my daughter was small, she and I planted another circular garden at the base of a Japanese maple that my husband and I put in near the house the year she was born.

It has wild geraniums in it and lily-of-the valley, and lots and lots of violets. I allow the violets go wild in there, as they will, but only there, and not in the other gardens around the house.

My daughter is turning twenty-two this year. The tree is nearly as tall as the roof of our house, and though it almost lost a limb in a snowstorm two years ago, it is beautiful. She, too, is beautiful.

They have grown up together and will continue to grow.

I'm learning that life involves at least as much waiting as gardening, maybe more.

I have also learned that I cannot control every outcome, no matter how carefully I plan and prepare.

IV.

I can, however, be attentive.

My brother Tom is gone, but if I am lucky, some of the lupine seed I brought back from the garden he loved in Maine will come up and survive the heat of a Connecticut summer.

My grandmother is gone, but maybe the forget-me-nots I transplanted from her garden in Pennsylvania will have survived the winter's cold.

I can be grateful.

I know that if I keep hiking to the top of the hill before the leaf buds on the trees open all the way, one day this spring I will find the knee-high umbrellas of the May-apples and the white waxy petals of the flowers underneath.

And I have learned that I can wait.

Preludes and Fugues

I.

In the little white house
with the moss-green braided rugs
and the armchair with soft green cushions,
and well-worn wooden arms,
where I curled up with my book,

Nana sat on the organ bench
with her back to me
and played Chopin and Bach.

It was not something we talked about.

She kept a clear glass bowl of blown-glass spheres
on top of the louvered bookcase —
translucent floats of sea green and foam,
from the lines for boats on the coast of Maine,

On the shelf nearby, leaning against each other,
scuffed cardboard sleeves held
her collection of orchestral music.

The turntable upon which she set the records
spun quietly under the needle arm.

We listened to all six Brandenburg Concertos,
one after another, over and over again,
but never tired of them.

In the winter, we pinned tissue-paper patterns
to red corduroy or flowered calico

and cut carefully along the thick black lines
to make matching dresses for my little sisters.

I knew that when the pieces of fabric were pinned
to each other, each pin had to run perpendicular
to the edge, so we could sew across them
on the machine by the bedroom window.

When the snow fell midwinter,
we rolled cookie dough flat
between sheets of waxed paper
and pressed stars into it.

It was my job to rub the baking sheet
with the inside of the wrapper
from a stick of butter before
we set the stars on it in rows.

She would dust the flour off her hands
on her apron, set the pot of cider
on the stove, turn the heat to low,
drop in a few cinnamon sticks,

then return to lift the records into place,
setting the needle gently down again
on the outer edge.

II.

When I was young and needed sanctuary
I walked up the hill and across a neighbor's yard
to visit Nana in the little white house
where she moved after my grandfather died.

When I appeared at her door
she would be playing the piano,
or sewing, or painting with pastels.

Other days she would be outside,
planting seeds in trays or digging
small holes for tulip bulbs in her garden.

Whatever she was doing I did with her.

Sometimes her table was set for a party,
fresh flowers in a vase, plans afoot for company.

In summer, she spread the yellow lacework
cloth from Italy underneath her best china,
served tiny cucumber sandwiches
on slices of thin white bread with butter.

Sprigs of mint floated among the ice cubes
in her pitcher of iced tea.

One day I found her sitting outside
at the table on the brickwork patio
with the newspaper in her lap.

She was crying over an article
she read about the little Negro girls
killed that Sunday morning at church in Alabama.

We talked for a long time about that.

III.

Nana treasured the thick yellow plates
with the blueberries painted on them,
reminders of her childhood in Maine.
Some of them were cracked now.

Helping to wash up after dinner,
I would find brown stains
at the bottom of every white china cup.

Years of adventures in the oven
had left the crooked cookie sheets
with blackened crumbs in every corner.

Nana couldn't see that anymore,
or could not be bothered, but it didn't matter.

Off to one side was her easel,
grey charcoal sticks in a little pile,
the soft erasers she used to blend her colors.

If the meat for dinner got a little burned
while she was painting a pastel,
she never seemed to mind.

Her favorite pastels were stubby,
each tip worn off at an angle.

I would study the exotic names of the colors
on the wrappers that were coming loose on each one:
Raw Umber, Burnt Sienna, and Prussian Blue.

I was sure that they were connected somehow
to the far-away places she had begun to visit.

IV.

When Nana came home from her trips
she brought dolls from every country back for me,
even from places she had not been to herself.

I dreamed about the places they had come from,
thought about those lives so different from mine.

The doll from Turkey wore a white woolen coat
and a black scarf wrapped around her head.
She carried a long spindle for wool in her left hand
and a stick with yarn wrapped around it in her right.

There was a whole set of books about children
from all over the world,
with blue bindings on the back and
black and white photographs of the children.

When Nana went away on a trip I would
read the stories in those books and imagine
her in all of those places so far away.

When she returned she shared her pastels with me.
Together we colored in the pictures of girls
wearing the traditional dress of their countries.

I did the patterns on the dresses —
the flowers on the embroidered trim
of the little Danish girl's apron,

the blue and white stripes
on the Dutch girl's skirt.

Nana did the shading on their braids
and cheeks, their lips and eyes,
and the tulips that the little Dutch girl held.

Her own paintings became pictures
of castles in the Swiss Alps, with edelweiss
on the mountainsides, and windmills in Holland.

She told me about seeing the statue in Copenhagen
of Hans Christian Andersen's Little Mermaid,
showed me pictures of houses in England
from Shakespeare's time.

V.

Every year Nana invited all the neighbors
to a Christmas Caroling party.

For weeks beforehand we measured cupfuls
of flour and sugar, teaspoons of salt and
tablespoons of butter for recipes for cookies
from the Joy of Cooking.

For the party we served cookies from Germany.
There were plates of Springerle with anise
and Lebchuken with honey.
Next to them were Krumkakes with almonds
and seed wafers from Scandinavia.

We decorated trays of gingerbread men

with raisins for eyes, buttons of red cinnamon candies,
and boots of white frosting.

Nana played carols on the organ from the Tasha Tudor book,
Take Joy! and all of us sang together, standing behind
her in a semi-circle, wearing sweaters she had brought
home from Norway, enough for all her twelve grandchildren.

VI.

When my Uncle David went to Rome on sabbatical
with my Aunt Rose Marie and their two small daughters,
I was invited to visit them with my Italian grandparents,
who were returning to Italy for the first time
since they had come to America as children.

For six weeks I was immersed in the landscape,
history, art and architecture of my Italian ancestry,
the colors in the paintings an awakening in themselves.

We lived in an apartment in the Trastevere section of Rome,
celebrated Easter at Santa Maria in Cosmedin, visited
the Pantheon, the Roman Forum and the Colosseum.

I slept in a bed decorated with Moroccan designs
and learned enough Italian to ask at the market
for blood oranges, fresh bread and cheese.

We took the train to Calabria, where my grandfather's
relatives invited us to dinner in a house built
into the mountainside in Sersale.

Then we took a ferry from Catanzaro to Sicily,

where we visited my grandmother's family
in a little town called Céfalu, near Mount Etna.

I stood in cathedrals and walked down the old streets
of many cities, with my aunt telling me stories about
the lives of the painters, the sculptors and the architects.

While I was away something happened
that would change my life. Nana was in a car accident.

Although she seemed fine at the time, the injury
may have led to the stroke she suffered later that year
the night before she was to accompany
a singer in a recital of opera arias.

When I returned from Italy everything was different.
Something was wrong with her.
We could not really talk.

I could not tell her about the harpsichord recital
I heard in Florence, or the frescoes on the ceiling
of the chapel in Padua, sky of lapis lazuli and stars of gold.

VII.

That next winter I sat at my Nana's sewing machine
making her a wine-red velvet gown
with long flowing sleeves, like the ones I had seen
in paintings of women of the Italian Renaissance.

I remember finishing the seams
with dark red silken binding tape,
knowing she might not live to wear the gown.

Nana was subdued, unfocused,
not so busy with what she loved.

I missed the tilt of her head
when she was lost in thought,
the way her fingers balanced over
the keys of the piano, the dust in the tray
at the bottom of her easel.

A graduate student moved into her house
to help out. We were not alone
together so much anymore.

I cannot remember much about that year.
I could not stand to see Nana so confused,
and began to grieve long before she left us.

Eventually she was moved into our house,
but whatever time we had left I wasted,
too upset by her condition to be with her.

My younger sister brought her drinks of water
and smoothed her blankets.

Nana was the person who knew me best,
the one I trusted to understand me.
She had given me so much of herself,
and now I could not help her.

I felt guilty
every time I walked past the door to her bedroom.

VIII.

It did not happen all at once, but little by little
I began losing my sense of who I was.
I spent more and more time alone,
wild with grief I did not know how to express.

The joyful little girl who tried so hard to be good
was now a young woman overwhelmed with
feelings she did not understand and could not control.

Nana was gone and I could not talk about it.

My parents thought I was just a teenager
like the children of their friends -
rebellious, secretive, silent.

They could not know how deep my self-hatred ran,
how I struggled with the feelings inside me.

I started wearing the same clothes to school every day,
refused to go to parties with my childhood friends,
distanced myself from the ones who had boyfriends.

Surrounded by people who loved me,
I judged them incapable of understanding me,
judged myself unworthy of their love.

Music became my sanctuary, books my companions.

I had started classical guitar lessons before Nana died,
listened over and over to Christopher Parkening
playing Bach on the album from my Aunt Rose Marie.

I practiced guitar in the dining room as though
my five siblings and my parents were not even there,
read Walt Whitman's *Leaves of Grass* and the book
Nana loved by Anne Morrow Lindberg, *Gift from the Sea.*

I discovered Euell Gibbons' *Stalking the Wild Asparagus,*
gathered plants from the woods with my friend Andrea,
and read Rachel Carson's *Silent Spring.*

I stood at the bus stop whistling the Gavottes
and Allemandes I loved from Bach's lute suites,
my heart breaking at the same time.

Even as I went on with my life,
getting involved in community projects,
growing as a musician, planting my gardens,
I had lost the deepest part of myself.

For many years, I let others take advantage of me.
Trying to prove to myself I would not abandon
those who were ill, I gave past all reason,
and ended by abandoning parts of myself.

At times the darkness was so deep that I had forgotten
who Nana was as well. I had lost her completely.

IX

In the end it was the music we had shared
on those quiet afternoons, my Nana and I,
that brought me back to myself and to her.

Drawn deeply into the *Lachrimae Pavane*

of John Dowland, Bach's *Six Suites for Cello*
and his *Mass in B Minor*, I discovered
an essential truth hidden within the pieces I loved.

The music that sustained me during the years
of forgetting was written by composers
who understood the darkness
and created beauty from it.

I learned that music could carry the weight
of the heaviest grief and transform it into joy.

Every year, with the friendships I made,
the music I played, and the time I spent
in the woods, and beside the ocean,
I grew stronger.

Over time, I remembered who Nana was
and what I had learned from her.

She knew that to live was to love, even if it hurt.
She knew that it is impossible to appreciate life
or create beauty without keeping your heart open.

I began to see that I had separated myself
from her during her last year and locked myself
into the darkness by trying to avoid
the pain of losing her.

The fall before my daughter was born,
I stood by the window in the kitchen
looking out at the trees at the edge of the woods
and knew —

having a child would mean I would love again,
and loving, risk losing the one I loved.

It was a risk I decided to take.
I do not regret it.

X.

Tonight I am surprised not to see
my mother's mother's face
looking back at me from the mirror
in the hallway by the door.

All the way home, alone on the dark
back roads, this late September evening,
a piano concerto by Rachmaninoff on the car radio,
I was lost in remembering her.

I have waited a long time to tell the story
of how my Nana and I wove our days together.
It is a story being revealed to me in the writing of it.

Little by little, the memories are returning.
Thankfully, I have her poems and paintings
to help me feel connected to her.

As soon as I learned to write,
Nana would let me copy my poems
into the grey book where she copied her poems.

I still have that book, written in her even hand,
with the poems I wrote as a child
written in the back of it, in careful script.
One of the earliest was "To a Candle."

Candle, candle burning bright,
in the dark and eerie night,
You mean hope and warmth and love,
as a symbol from above.

Against the background
of dark fear,
to those who hold you,
friends seem near.

XI.

I read the poems she wrote about how much
she missed my grandfather, and their love for each other.
She wrote many poems about the difficulty
of going on with her life after losing him.

Poems about her childhood,
her dreams and disappointments,
her puzzlement and grief over the distance
between her and her only sister.

Poems with sayings from her father,
nearing his hundredth birthday, and descriptions
of the lives of her children and her grandchildren.

And this poem about me,
titled "Laura Anne."

One morning I felt lonely,
And hours stretched far ahead,
When a little girl came,
Dancing in my room.

Her eyes were so bright and merry,
Wild flowers were in her hand,
That sunshine at once
Took the place of gloom.

In another one, about waving goodbye to me
when I left with my father's parents
to visit Italy, she wrote,

Only yesterday a little girl
Playing with dolls at home.
My throat felt tight as I kissed her goodbye
I could have shed a few tears
Without much try.

She didn't know I felt this way
As I tried to look at her quite gay,
As red-caped and smiling she flew away.
"To Rome with Love" I managed to say."

XII.

Nana did not begin painting with pastels
until after my grandfather died.

In her poem "Pastels" she wrote
that she had been told she could not draw,
but, in verse two, she says,

Years went by in longing,
And she didn't dare to try,
Until one bold and daring day,
Her pastels became blue sky.

She wrote that in 1965, the year I turned ten.
By the time I turned fifteen, she was gone.

The pastels that Nana did the year before she died
are blurred, as her vision must have been
after the stroke.

In one, soft pink peonies and tall blue delphinium
are standing in a green vase.
In the center, a yellow rose.

I see that painting every day and think of her.

Forty-five years have passed since she was buried
in the velvet dress I made for her,
never having worn it before that.

I think now that she must have understood
my adolescent anguish over her long decline
and forgave me for it. I imagine she would
encourage me to try to forgive myself.

I am nearly as old now as she was
when she lost her husband.
I am using everything I learned from her
about how to live, and how to live alone.

The wall hanging Nana designed of a tree
with a twisted trunk and many-colored leaves
hangs on the wall above my piano.

She taught her grandchildren how to use
woolen thread and embroidery needles
so they could each add a leaf to it.

I think she would like knowing that it is here.

Today I would like to show her my garden,
my music room, the trees outside my window,
put a fire in the woodstove and make her a cup of tea.

I would love to invite her to sit on the piano bench,
get out her old books of music, and play Chopin again.

I want to ask her to tell me about her life —
her childhood on the coast of Maine
in the days of sailing ships and sea captains.

I want to introduce her to my daughter,
another musician and poet, and listen
as they enjoy each other's company.

I want to give her time to write a new poem
on the blank pages in the back of this book of mine.

POSTLUDE

Of Answers and Questions

Each time one of my questions
reaches the mature perfection
        of a midsummer leaf,

it falls from my branch of thoughts
into a swift stream of confusion
        and I lose it.

So, having lost all of my questions
how can I hope to find the answer?

Searching still . . .
I find nothing but other seekers.

I wonder if they know any better
what they are looking for.

Sometimes I think the answer must be
        everywhere, pervading everything,

and were I to look hard enough
        deep into the center of a flower
        far away between the stars
        I would find it.

written at age 14, a year before my Nana died

Rondo for Wood Thrush and Salamander

I. Overture

Begin at the end of the long season of snow and ice.
Wake with the birds that welcome the early dawn.

Find the walking stick you left last fall leaning
against a tree at the bottom of the hill.

Walk deep into the woods, where sunlight streams
through the branches of trees, leaf buds barely visible.

Mourn the birches that came down in the winter,
admire the way they have begun to loosen their bark.

It is the season of skunk cabbage and fiddlehead ferns.
The woods are waiting. It is time. Listen!

II. Rondo

When the melting snow carves channels
down the steepest section of the rocky path
and softens the ground all the way to the brook,

the horses' hooves sink deep into the mud
on the trail at the bottom of the hill.

 Tread the muddy trail with care,
  watch the ground beneath your feet.

 The woods are coming back to life,
  for it will be, as it has always been,
 a time for listening. Listen!

When the acorns begin to unzip their brown jackets,
showing glimpses of scarlet beneath, you will find
the white stars low beside the trail,
and the dark red trillium at the top of the hill.

Then you will know the time is near. Listen!

One day soon, three notes of silver will float
from a high branch, followed a by a rapid trill,
a moment of silence, and another spiral of silver notes.
The wood thrush has returned, singing.

> Tread the muddy trail with care,
>   watch the ground beneath your feet.

> The woods are coming back to life,
>   for it will be, as it has always been,
> a time for listening. Listen!

The thrush sings three quicker notes, not audible before,
followed by a longer trill and the beginning of a new song,
leaping higher and dipping down to finish
with a *port de voix*, an ornament favored
by composers in France before the Revolution.

The next day, the song of the first wood thrush
is answered by a companion singing higher up the hillside.
The two begin trading questions and answers,
like Gabrieli's antiphonal choirs sounding from one balcony
to another across the majestic nave of San Marco.

Tread the muddy trail with care,
    watch the ground beneath your feet.

The woods are coming back to life,
    for it will be, as it has always been,
a time for listening. Listen! And look!

Along the wettest path, where the water
runs beneath the layers of oak leaves, one by one,
the bright orange salamanders appear.

Each miniature flame pauses in climbing position
with its legs outstretched, believing itself invisible.
Could the salamanders be listening too?

Count your steps as you climb the hill. Look down.
The day after a heavy rain, you will find
a tiny orange salamander at every seventh step.

Tread the muddy trail with care,
    watch the ground beneath your feet.

The woods are coming back to life,
    for it will be, as it has always been,
a time for listening. Listen! Listen!

ABOUT THE AUTHOR

The eldest of six children born to an Italian-American father with the passionate temperament of a reformer and a mother deeply rooted in the optimism and pragmatism of her New England ancestors, Laura Mazza-Dixon grew up close to her grandparents in State College, Pennsylvania, embraced by their family traditions and keenly aware of the differences between them. Music, the life of the spirit, political activism, poetry, and the natural world have been her passions. She plays and teaches both guitar and viola da gamba, with a particular interest in traditional Celtic, Renaissance and Baroque music. She has been a guiding spirit behind the Bruce Porter Memorial Music Series and the Granby Family Dance Series in Granby, CT. Religious and meditative traditions have been at the heart of Laura's life since childhood, always viewed through the lens of her questioning spirit and inspiring her to promote social and political change. From her earliest days, she has been a poet and a promoter of poetry, writing with great energy and organizing the Poetry at the Cossitt series. Recently, she has also organized Courageous Conversations on Race poetry workshops in Granby, where she lives and tends to the gardens and plantings that have been a mainstay in her life. In what little is left of her spare time, she hikes the woods of Connecticut with Tuddy, her guardian canine spirit, and relishes the life of coastal Maine, the ancestral home of her mother's family.

This book is set in Garamond Premier Pro, which had its genesis in 1988 when type-designer Robert Slimbach visited the Plantin-Moretus Museum in Antwerp, Belgium, to study its collection of Claude Garamond's metal punches and typefaces. During the mid-fifteen hundreds, Garamond—a Parisian punch-cutter—produced a refined array of printing types that combined an unprecedented degree of balance and elegance, for centuries standing as the pinnacle of beauty and practicality in type-founding. Slimbach has created an entirely new interpretation based on Garamond's designs and on compatible italics cut by Robert Granjon, Garamond's contemporary.

To order additional copies of this book
or other Antrim House titles, contact the publisher at

Antrim House
21 Goodrich Rd., Simsbury, CT 06070
860.217.0023, AntrimHouse@comcast.net
or the house website (www.AntrimHouseBooks.com).

•

On the house website
in addition to information on books
you will find sample poems, upcoming events,
and a "seminar room" featuring supplemental biography,
notes, images, poems, reviews, and
writing suggestions.